Fourth Position for the Viola

by Cassia Harvey

CHP270

©2017 by C. Harvey Publications All Rights Reserved.

www.charveypublications.com

Fourth Position for the Viola

by Cassia Harvey

A. First Shifting on the A String

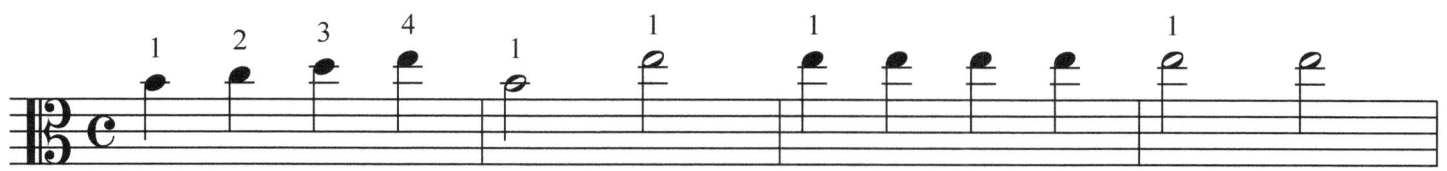
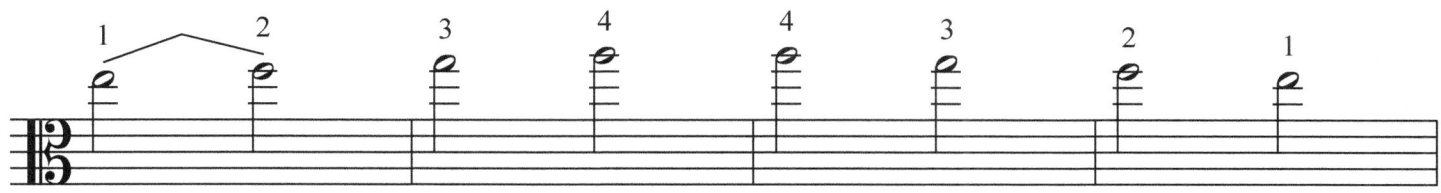
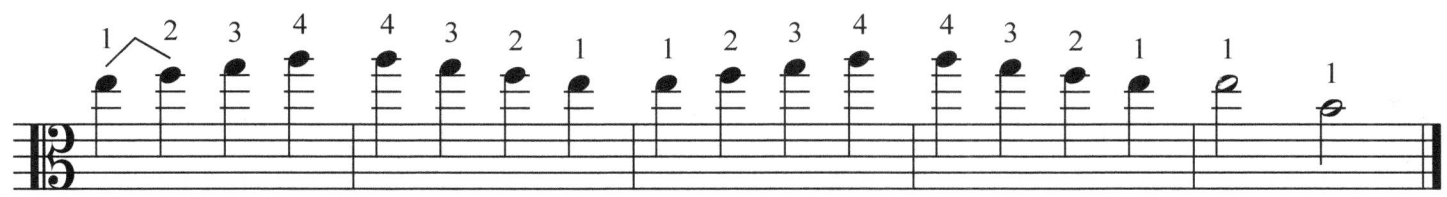

B. First Shifting on the D String

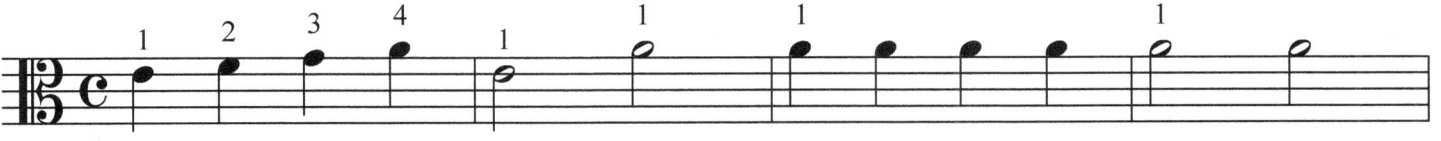
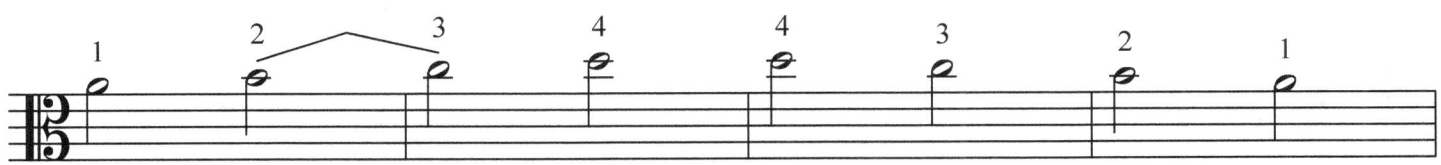

©2017 C. Harvey Publications All Rights Reserved.

C. First Shifting on the G String

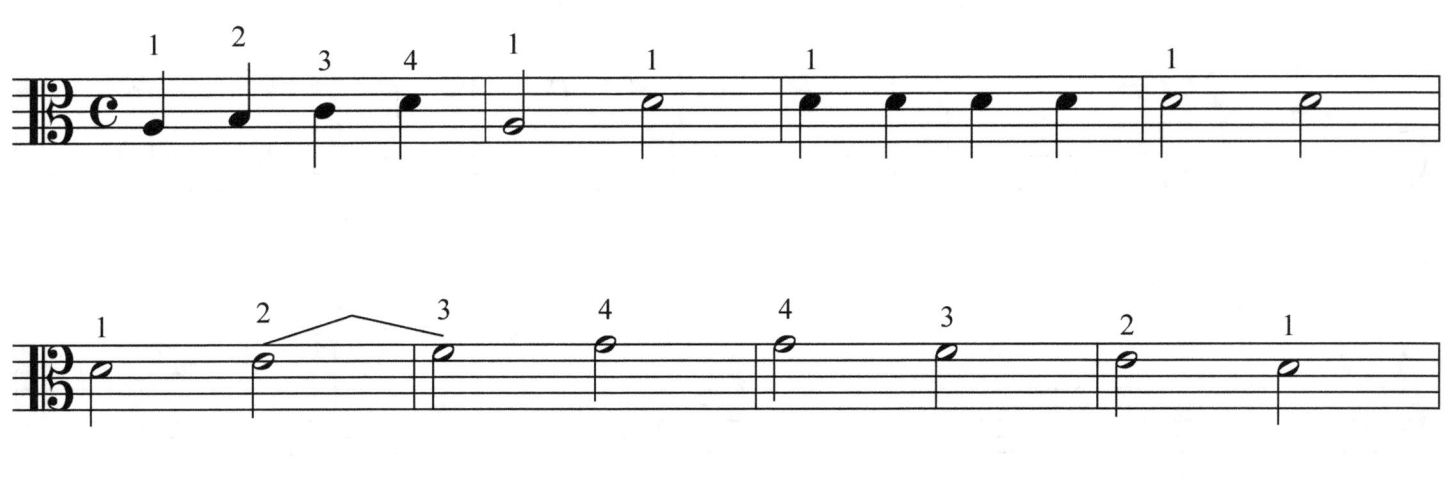

D. First Shifting on the C String

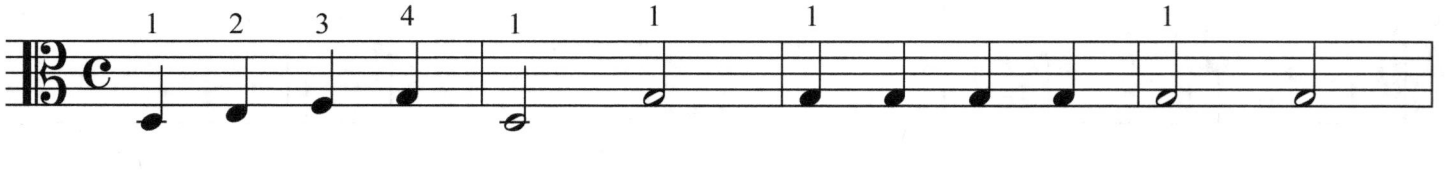

Fourth Position for the Viola

1. First Fingers in Fourth Position

2. Fourth Position Across Strings

3. Fourth Position on the G String

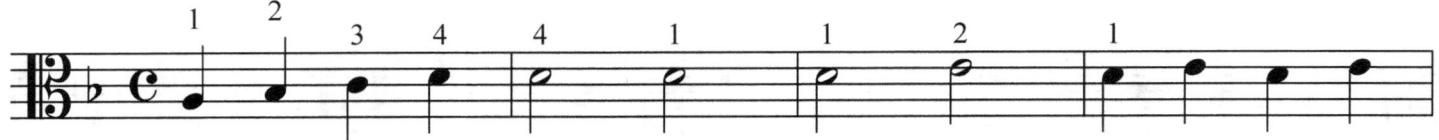

4. Shifting to Fourth Position

Fourth Position for the Viola

5. Little Dance

6. Harvest Chant

7. First to Fourth Fingers on the G String

8. Fourth Position Spaces on the G String

Fourth Position for the Viola

9. A Plaintive Tune

10. Tarantella

©2017 C. Harvey Publications All Rights Reserved.

Fourth Position for the Viola

11. Using Four Fingers

12. Finger Exercise

Fourth Position for the Viola

13. Jaunty Shifting

14. Waltz

Fourth Position for the Viola

15. Crossing Strings to First Finger

16. Patterns of Three

Fourth Position for the Viola

17. Tango

16. Jig

19. More Fourth Position Notes on the A String

20. Shifting from Third Finger

Shifting Diversion 1

Shifting Diversion 2

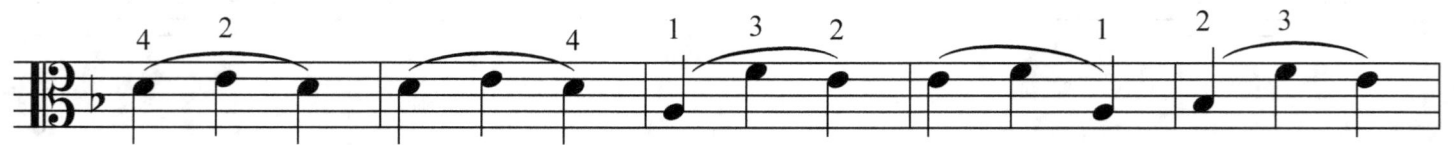

Fourth Position for the Viola

Shifting Diversion 3

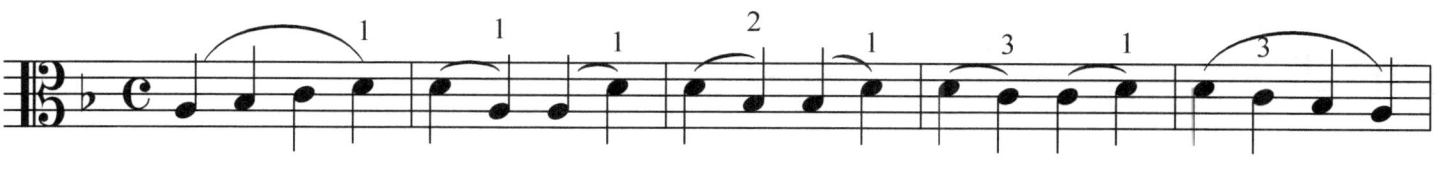

©2017 C. Harvey Publications All Rights Reserved.

23. Crossing Strings

24. Finger Pattern

©2017 C. Harvey Publications All Rights Reserved.

Fourth Position for the Viola

25. Bergamask

26. Reaching Across to the C String

27. The Notes on the C String

Fourth Position for the Viola

28. Mazurka

29. Truculence

30. Crossing to the C String

31. When to Shift and When to Cross

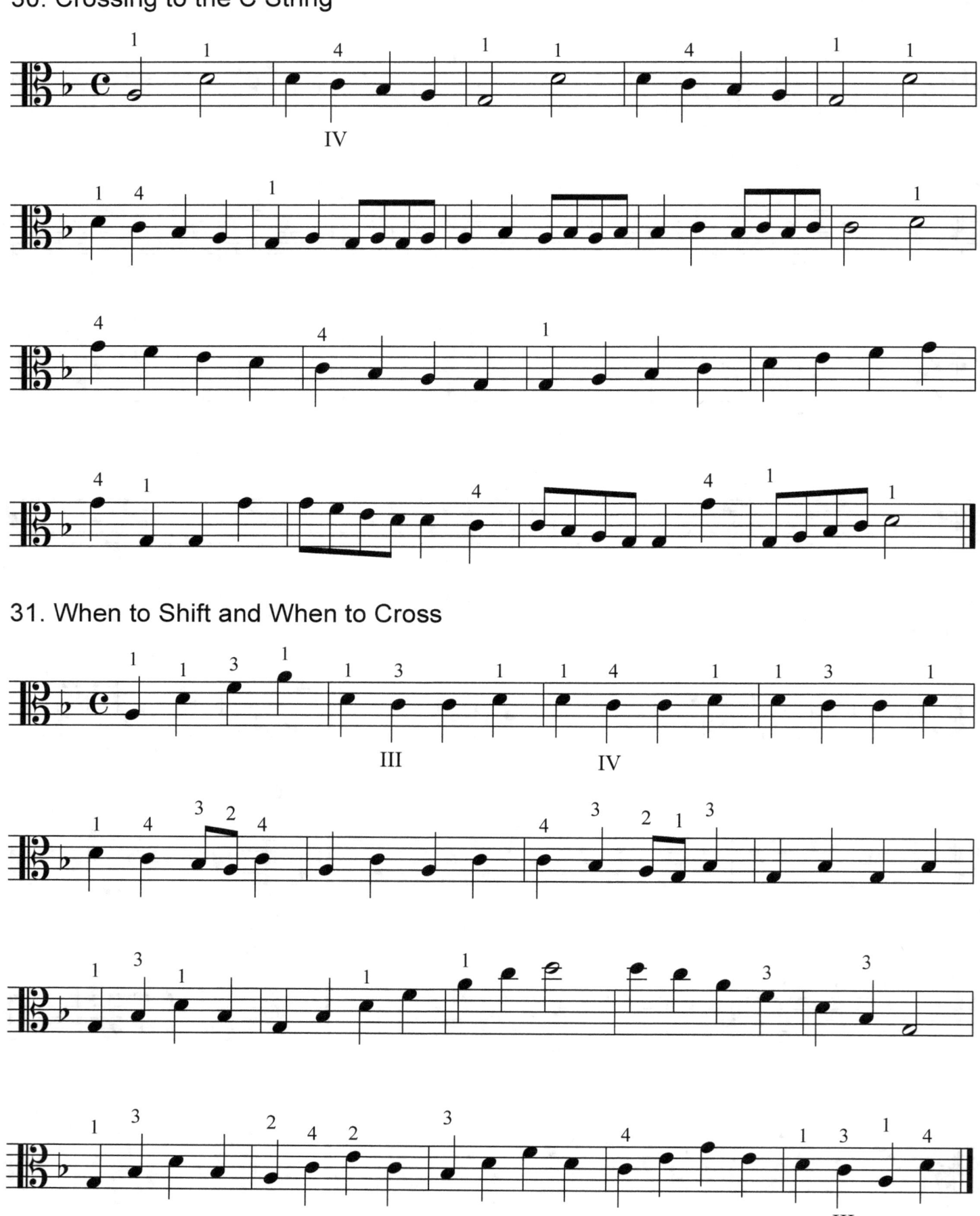

Fourth Position for the Viola

32. Chaconne

33. Matachin

34. The Notes on the A String

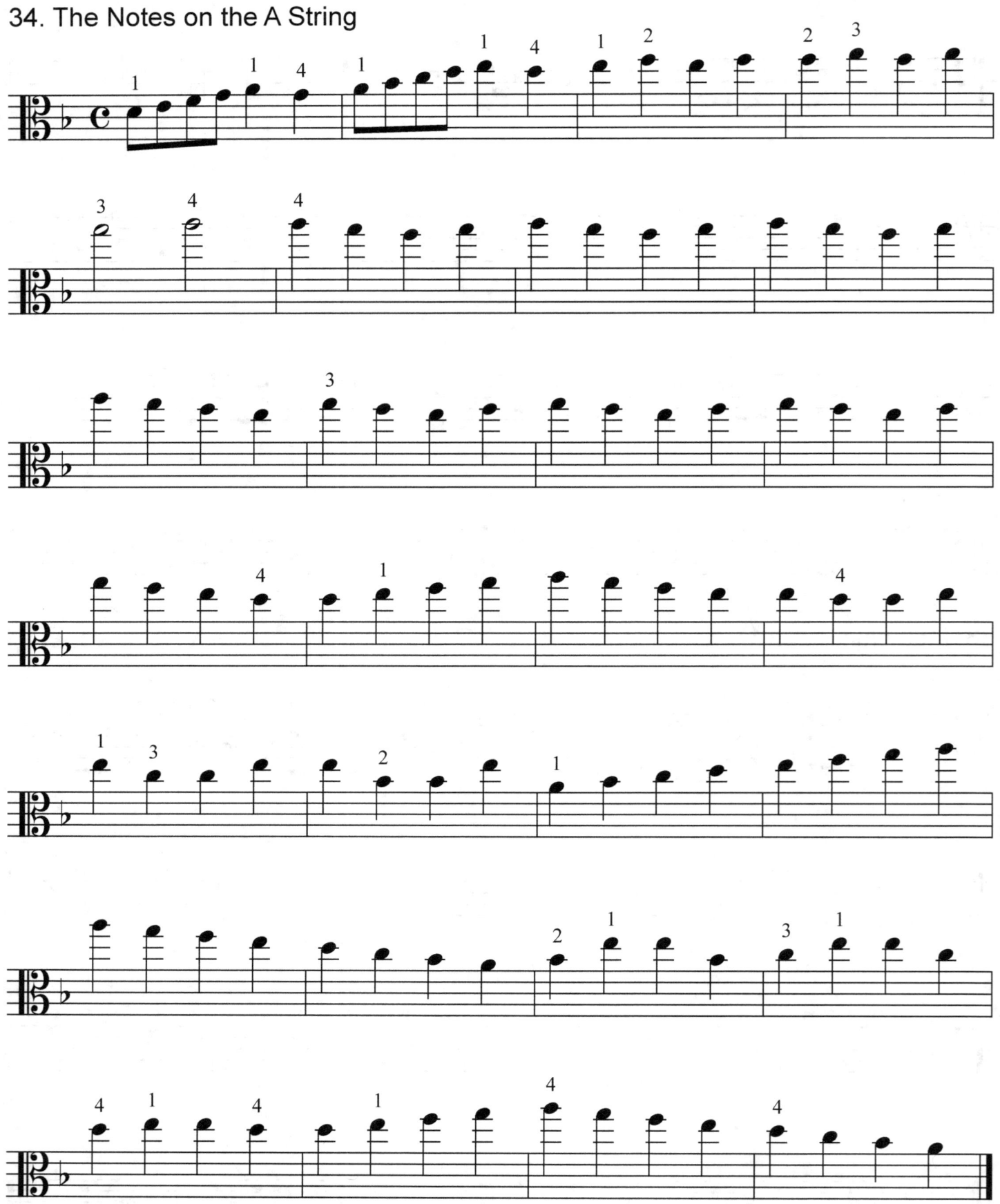

Fourth Position for the Viola

35. Tempo Giusto

36. Kazachoc

©2017 C. Harvey Publications All Rights Reserved.

Fourth Position for the Viola

37. Crossing to the A string

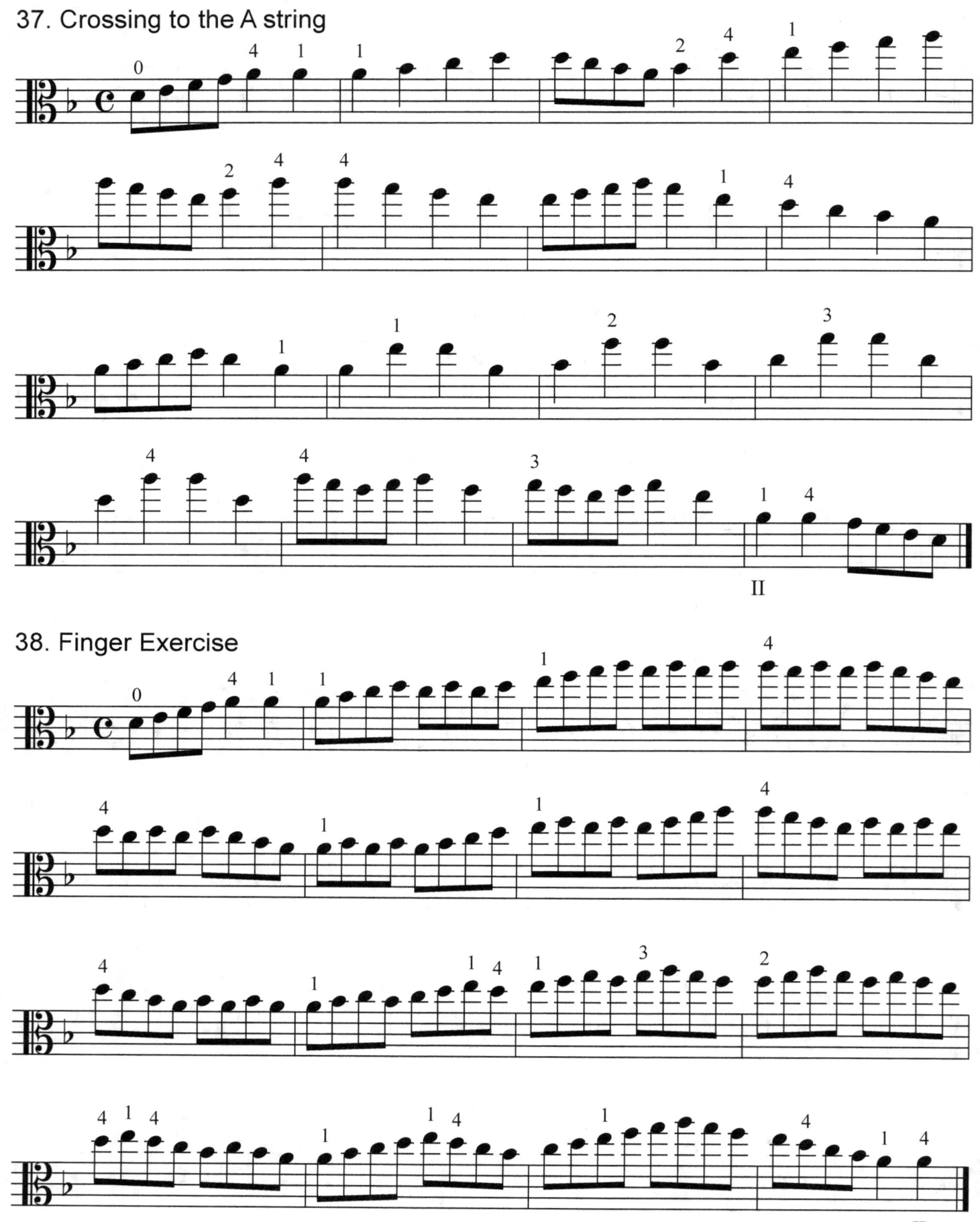

38. Finger Exercise

Fourth Position for the Viola

39. Tempo Comodo

40. Reel

41. Little Scales

42. Crossing Strings

Fourth Position for the Viola

43. Misterioso

44. Semplice

45. Shifting on the C String

46. Shifting on the G String

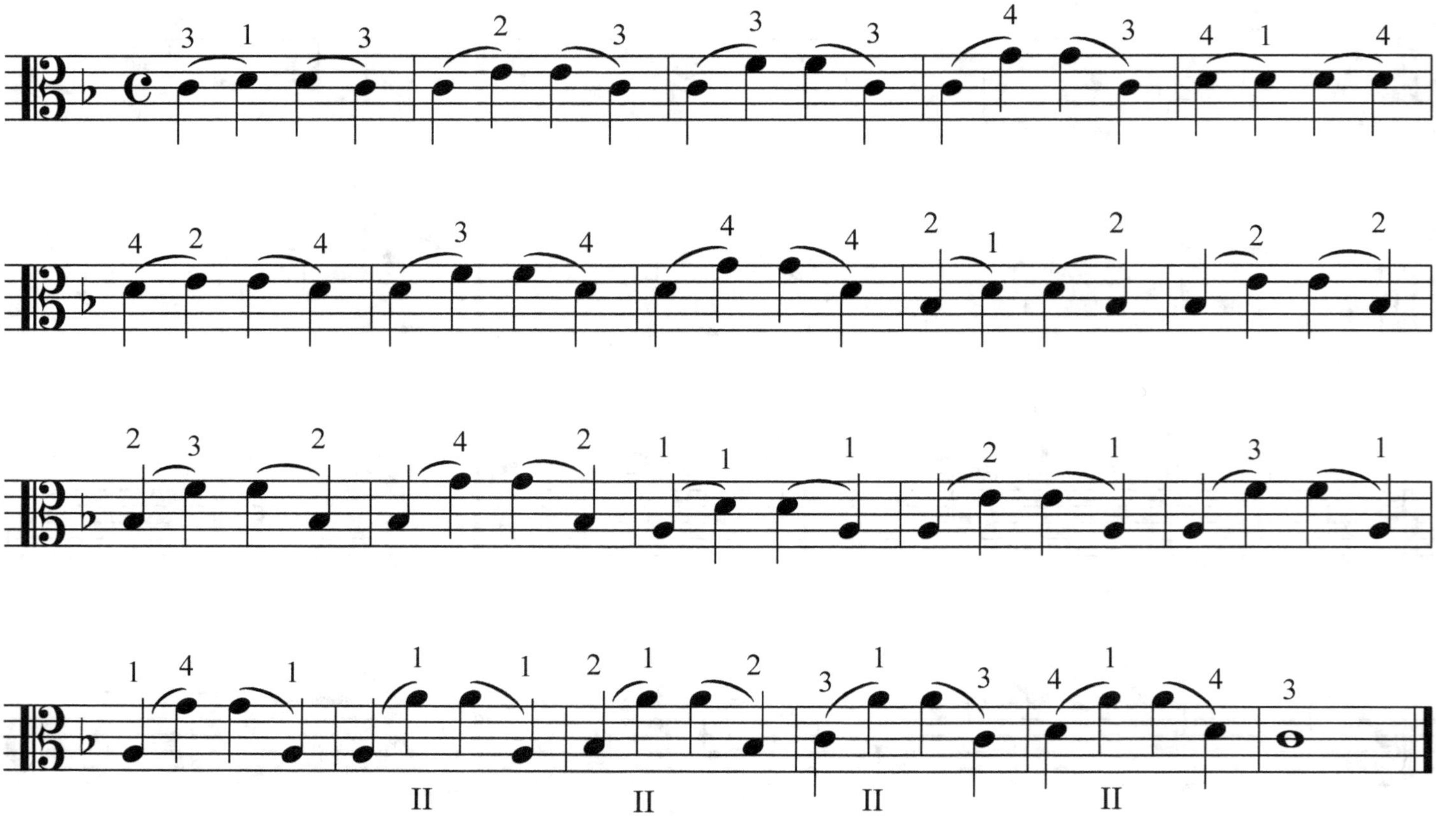

Fourth Position for the Viola

47. Sostenuto

48. Affetuoso

49. Shifting on the D String

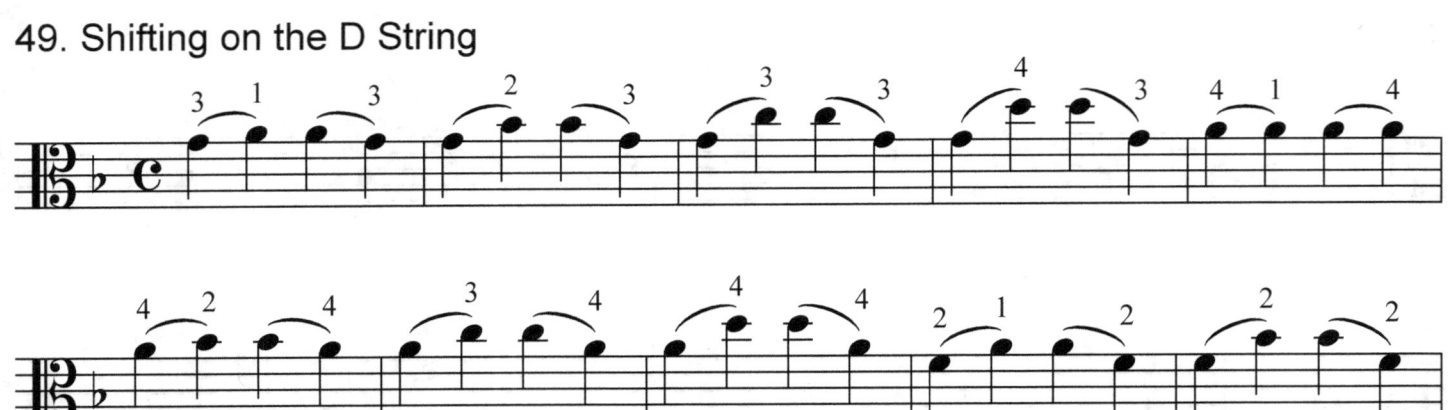

50. Shifting on the A String

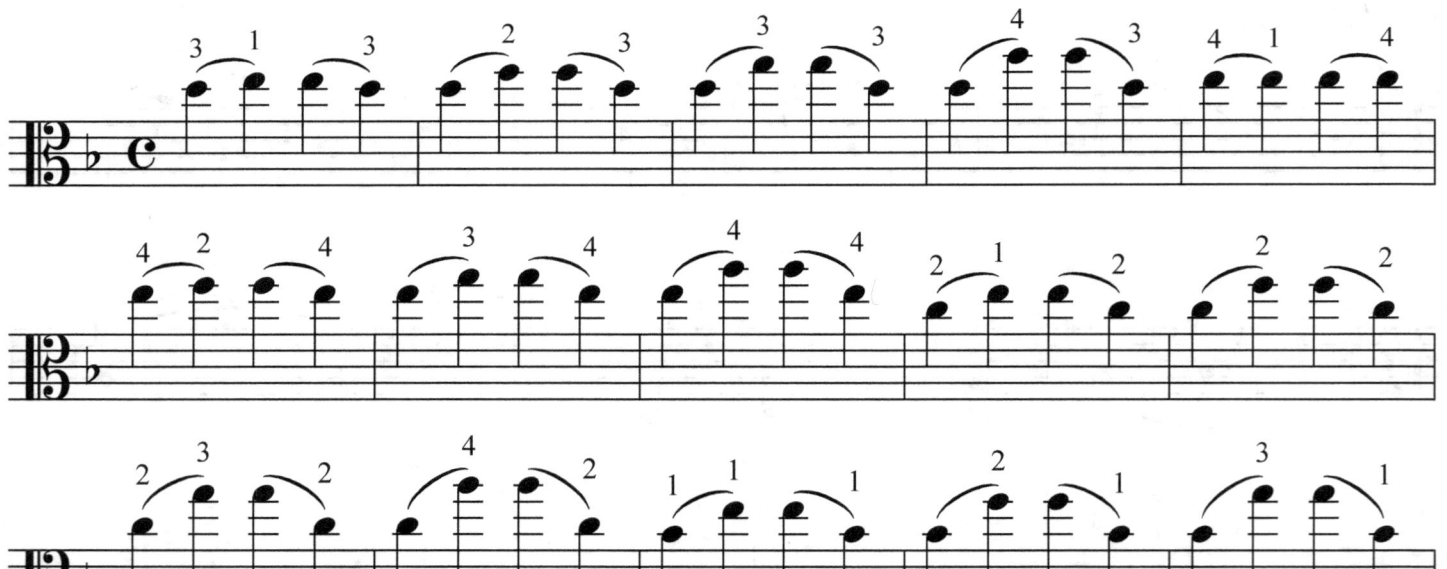

Fourth Position for the Viola

51. Grazioso

52. Cantabile

©2017 C. Harvey Publications All Rights Reserved.

53. C Major

54. High and Low 3rd Finger

Fourth Position for the Viola

55. Portugese Folk Song

56. Rameau's Minuet

Fourth Position for the Viola

59. Le Couppey's Study

60. Keller's Morceau Paysane

61. Scale and Broken Thirds in C Major

62. Arpeggio Patterns in C Major

Fourth Position for the Viola

63. Energico

64. Dolce

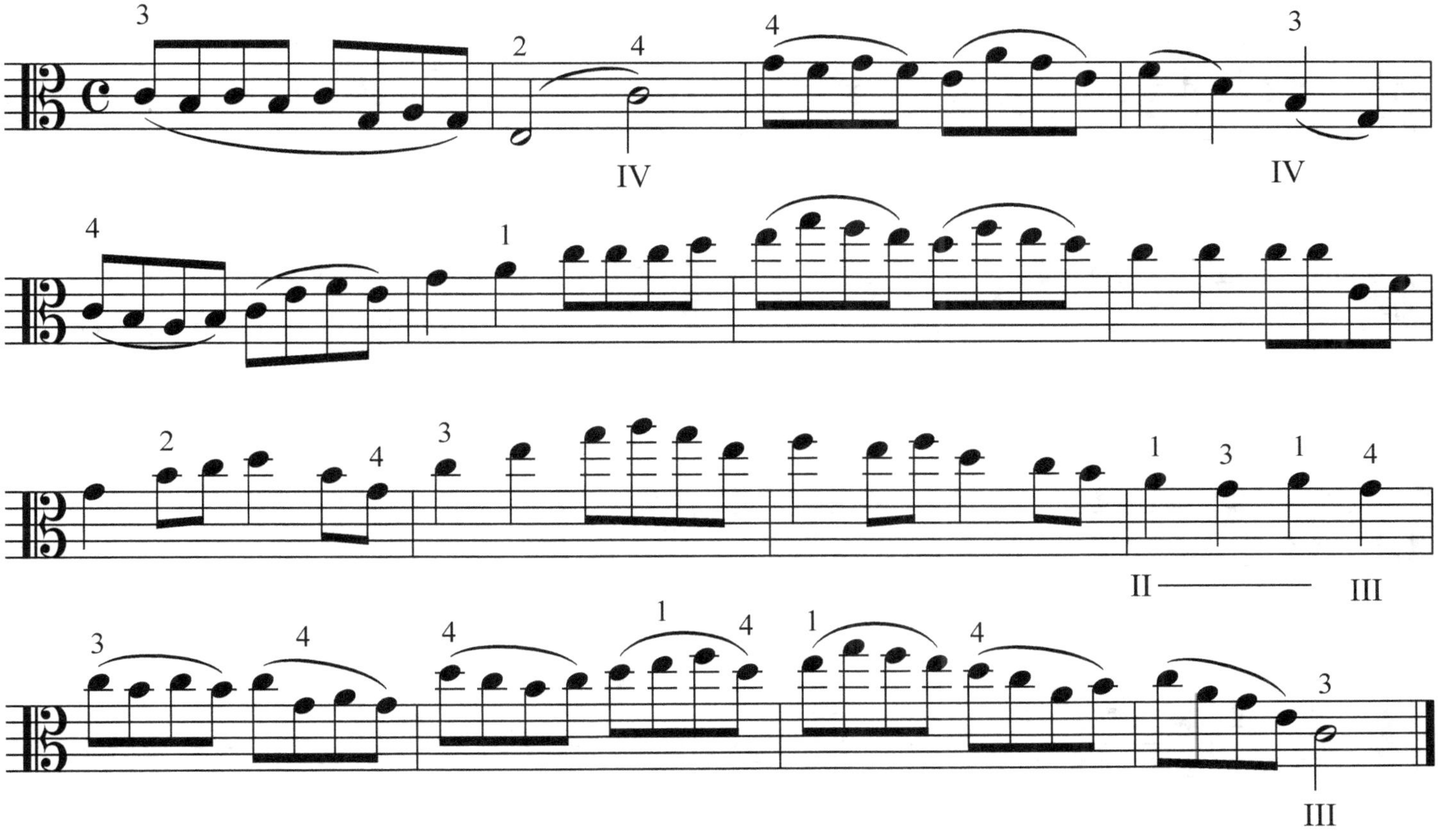

65. G Major

66. Patterns in G Major

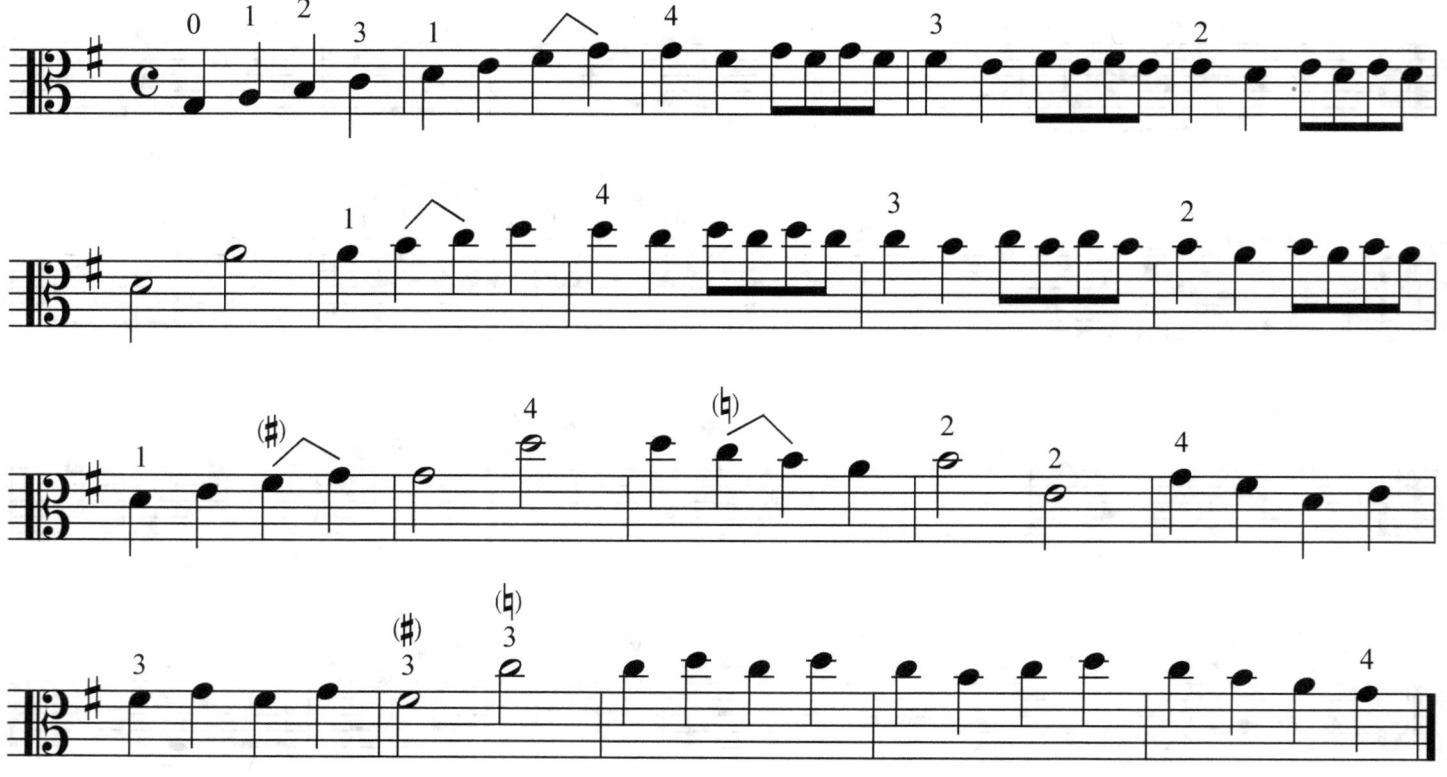

Fourth Position for the Viola

67. Ziganka

68. Dance Reel

Fourth Position for the Viola

71. Loure

72. Gavotte

73. Finger Exercise in G Major

74. Coming Down

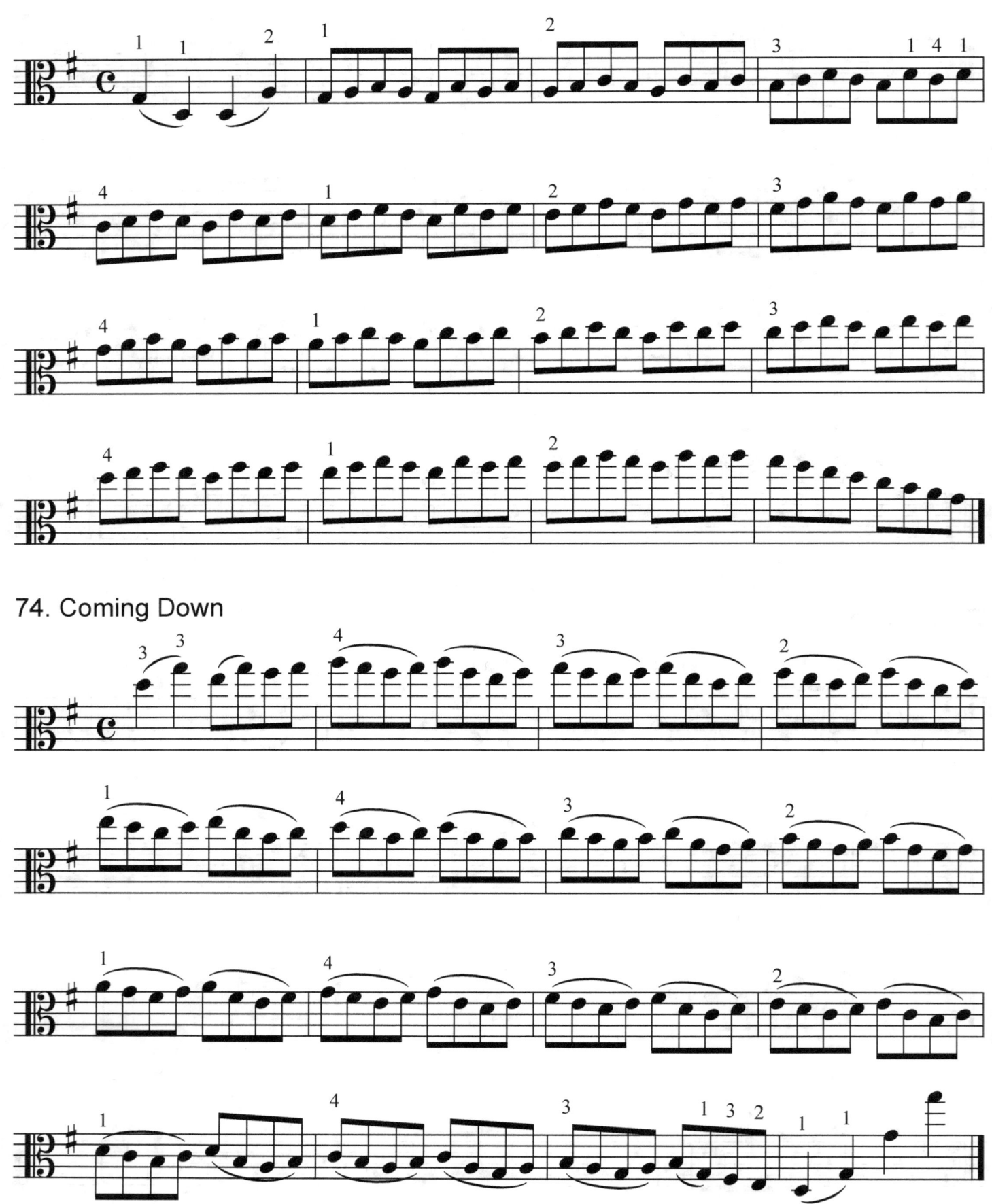

75. Kozeluch's Sonata

76. Contradance

Fourth Position for the Viola

77. D Major

78. C♯ and G♯ in D Major

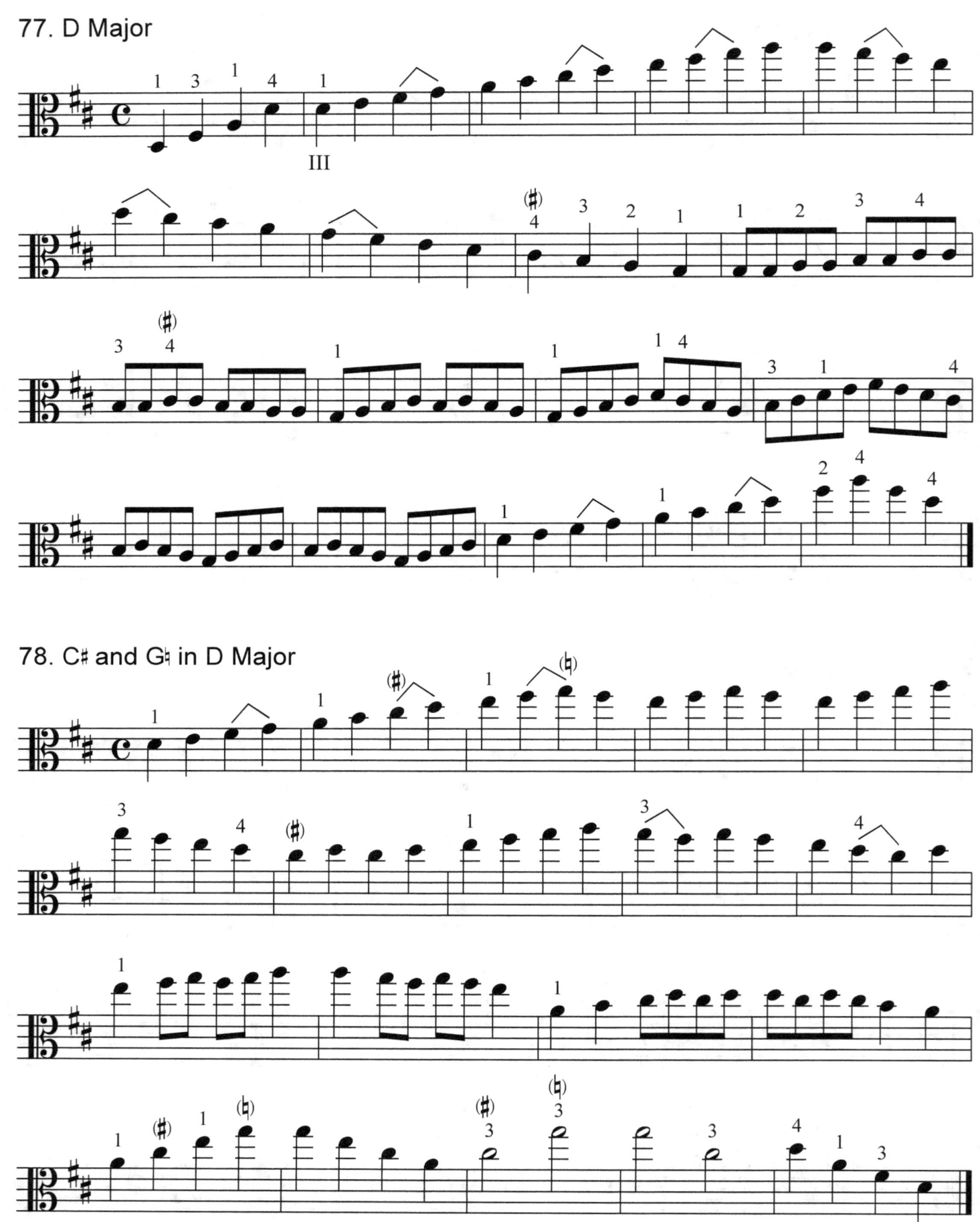

©2017 C. Harvey Publications All Rights Reserved.

Fourth Position for the Viola

79. Vivace

80. Bast's English Dance

Fourth Position for the Viola

83. Brillante

84. Giga

85. Broken Thirds in D Major

86. Skipping Notes in D Major

Fourth Position for the Viola

87. Varsovienne

88. Zoppetto

©2017 C. Harvey Publications All Rights Reserved.

Fourth Position for the Viola

89. B♭ Major

90. Low First Finger E♭ in B♭ Major

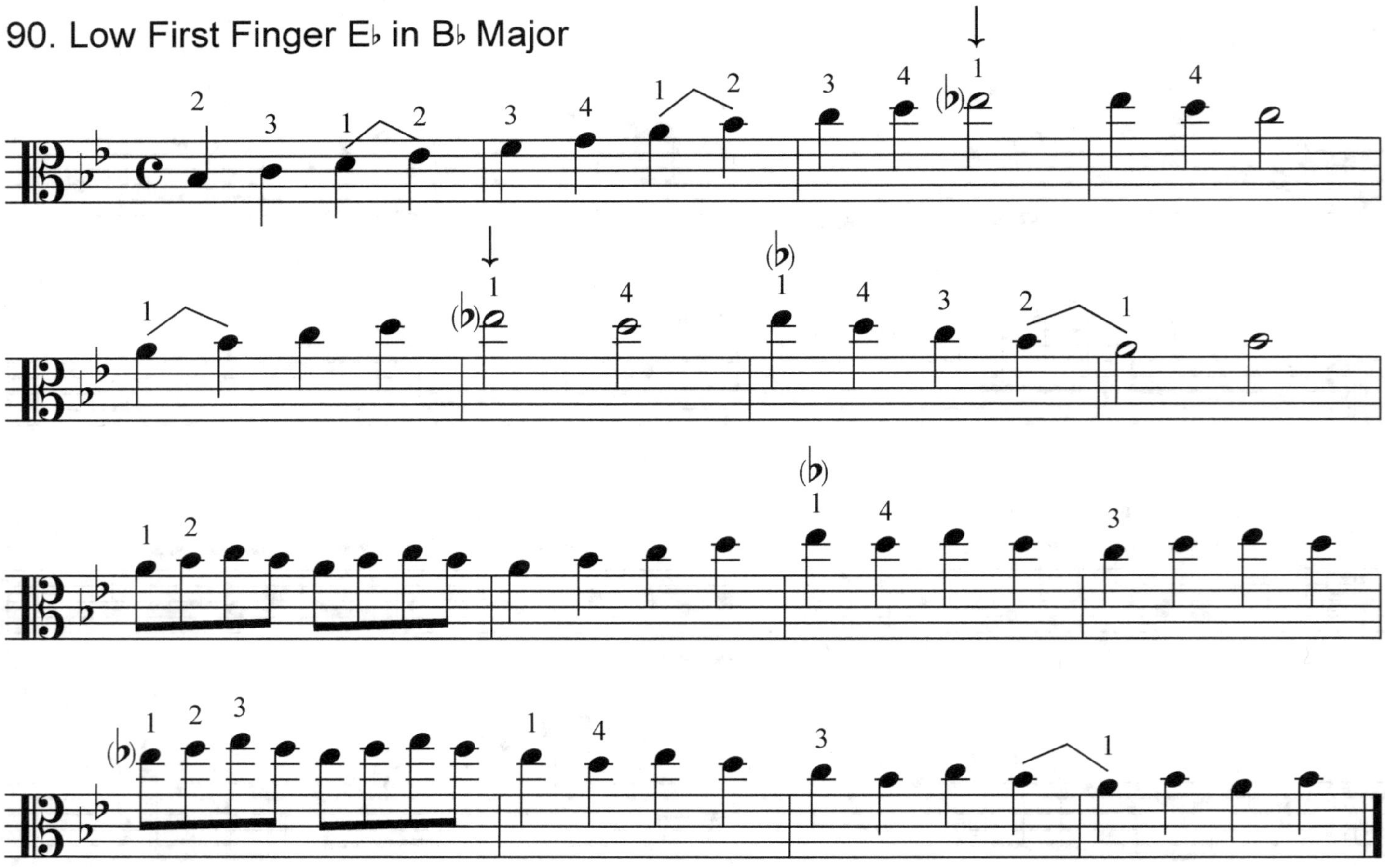

Fourth Position for the Viola

91. Giocoso

92. Soave

Fourth Position for the Viola

95. Capriccioso

96. Affabile

©2017 C. Harvey Publications All Rights Reserved.

97. A♮ to E♭

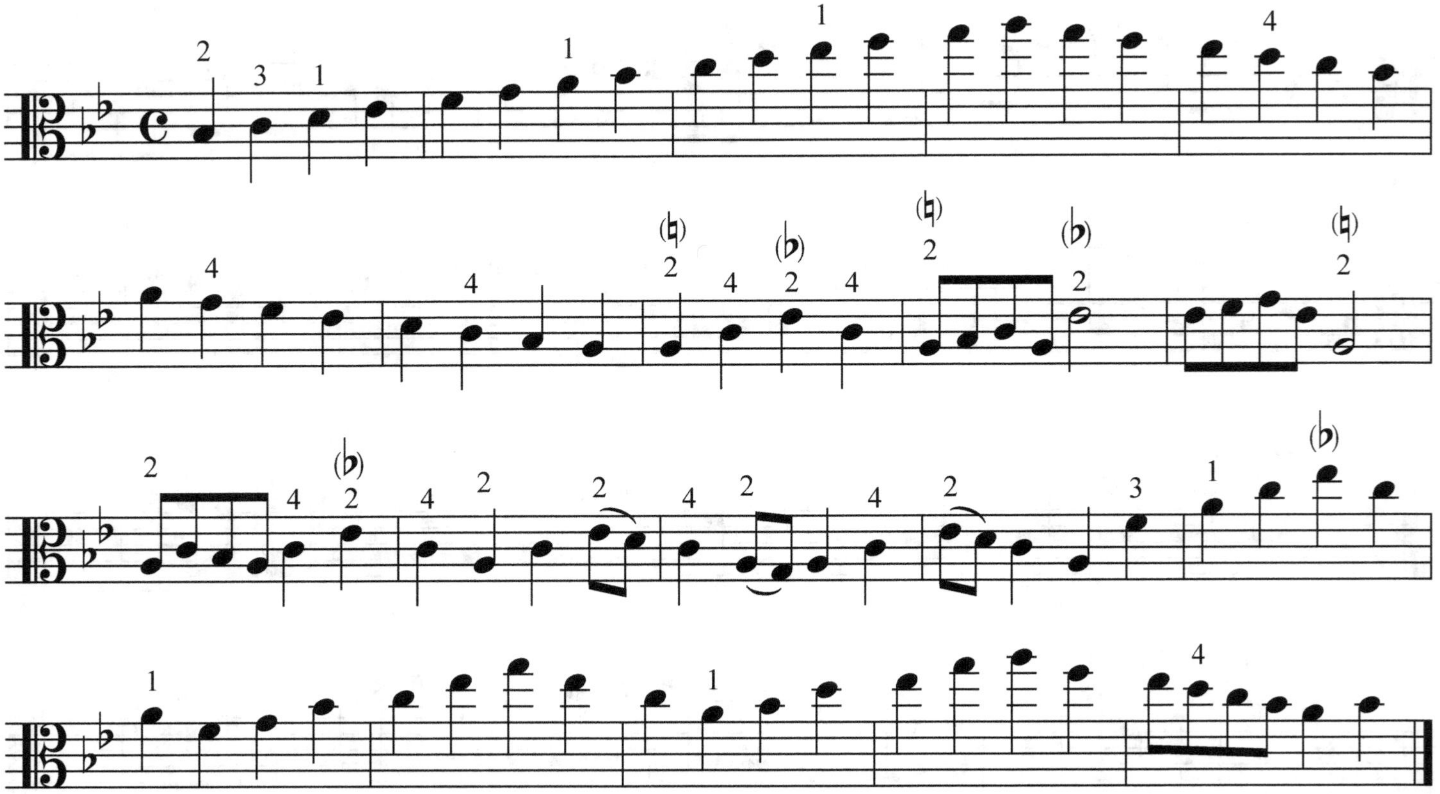

98. Crossing Strings and Shifting

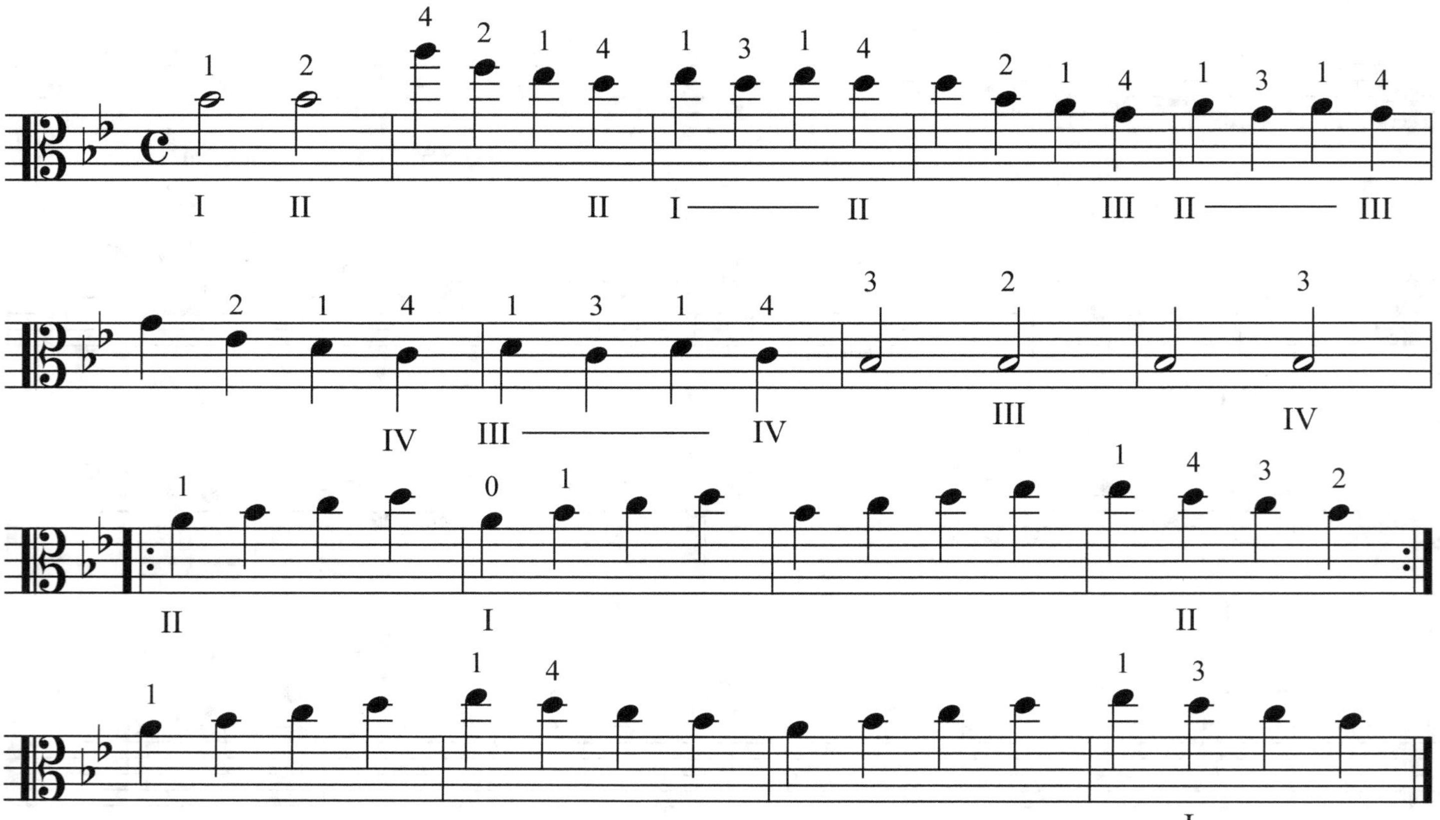

Fourth Position for the Viola

99. Piangevole

100. Scherzo

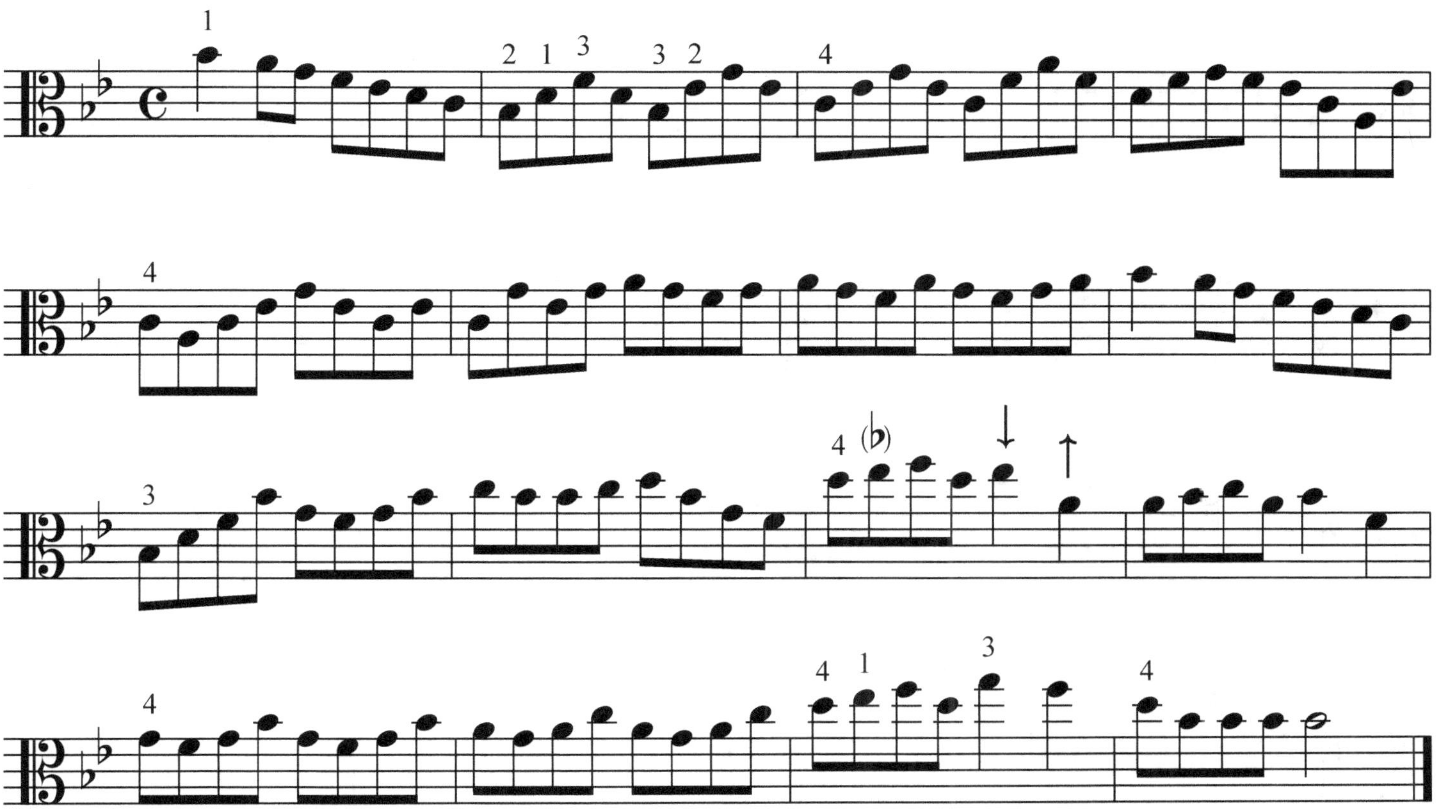

101. E♭ Major

102. Crossing Strings in E♭ Major

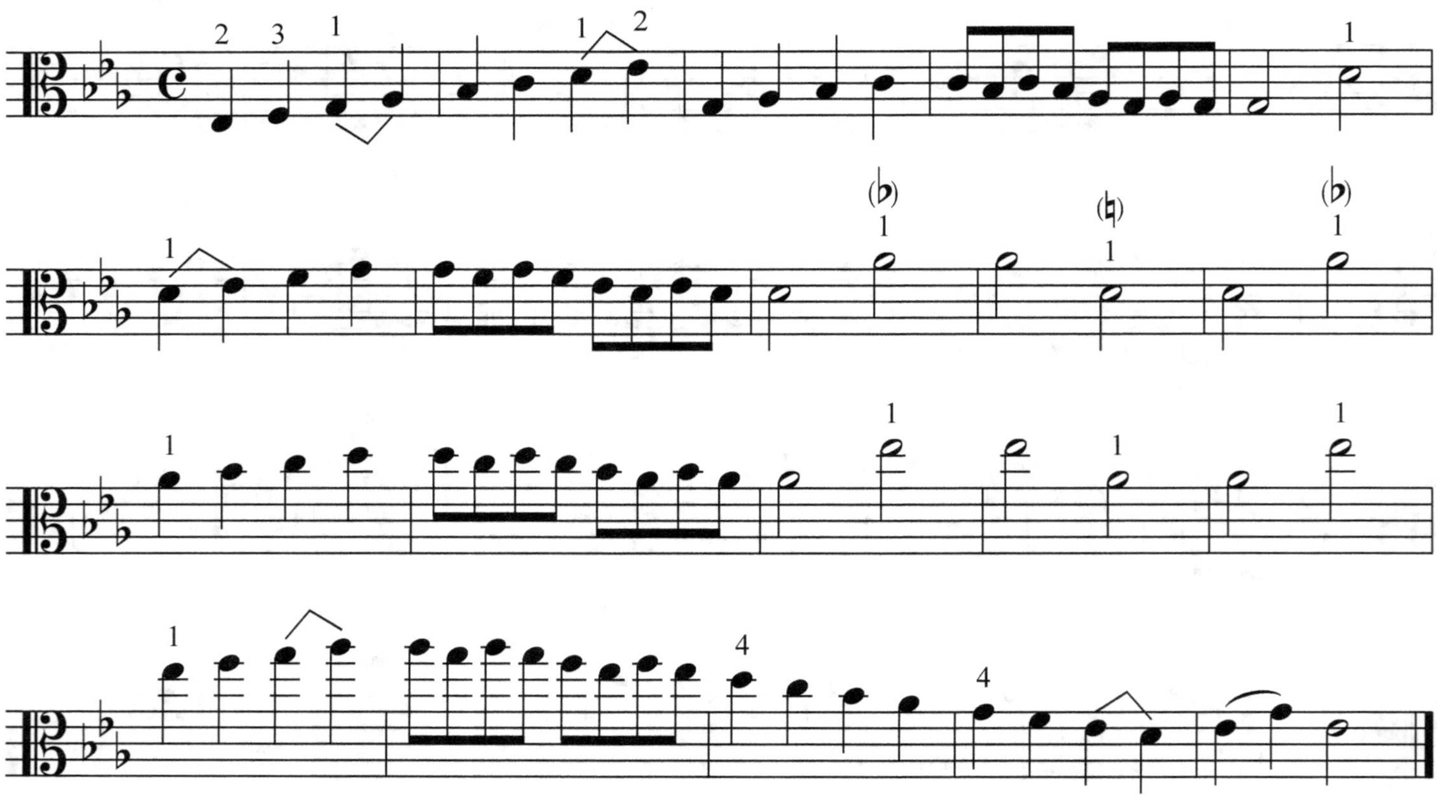

Fourth Position for the Viola

103. Lusigando

104. Sospirando

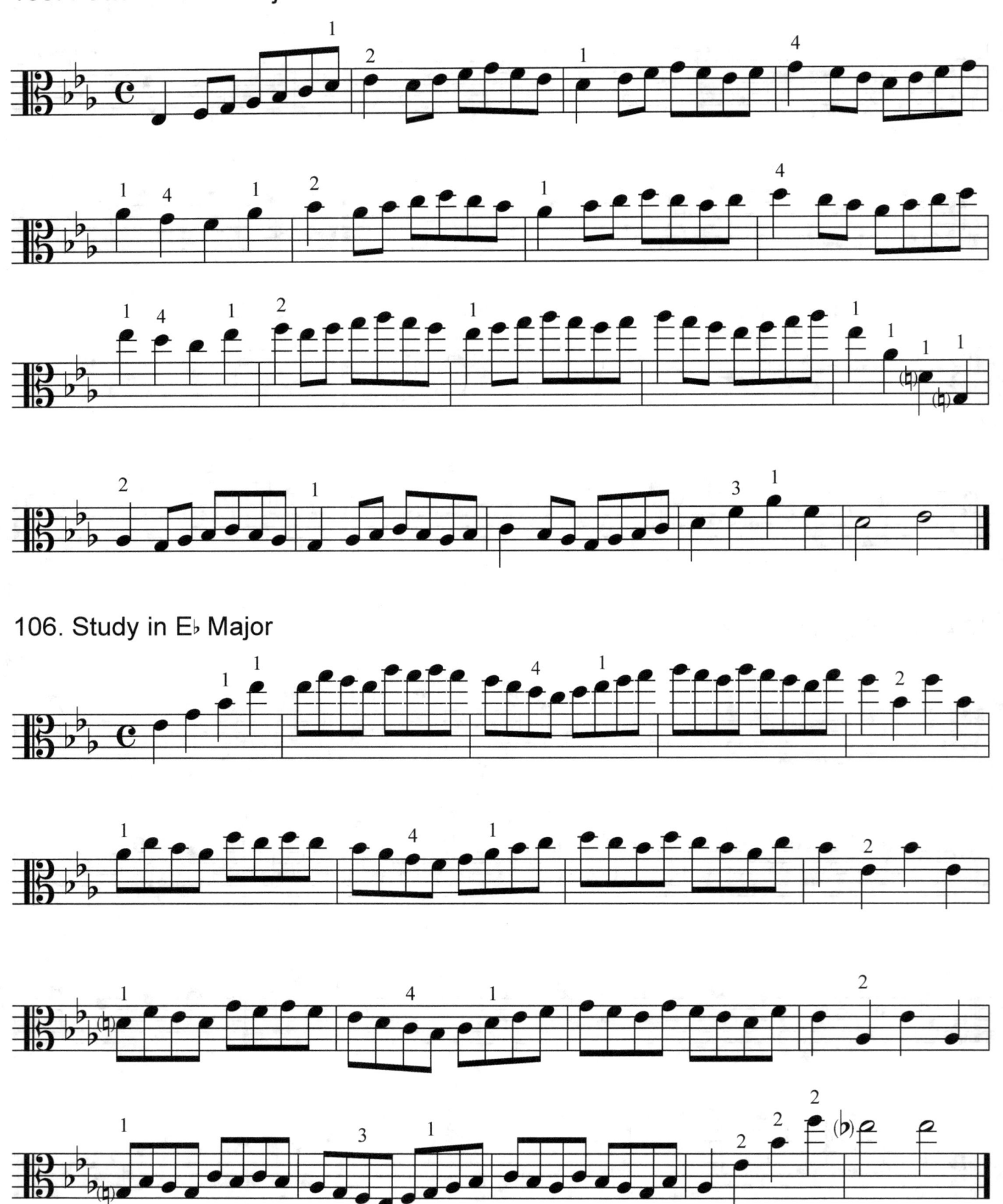

Fourth Position for the Viola

107. Tangential

108. Ritmico

109. Across Strings in E♭ Major

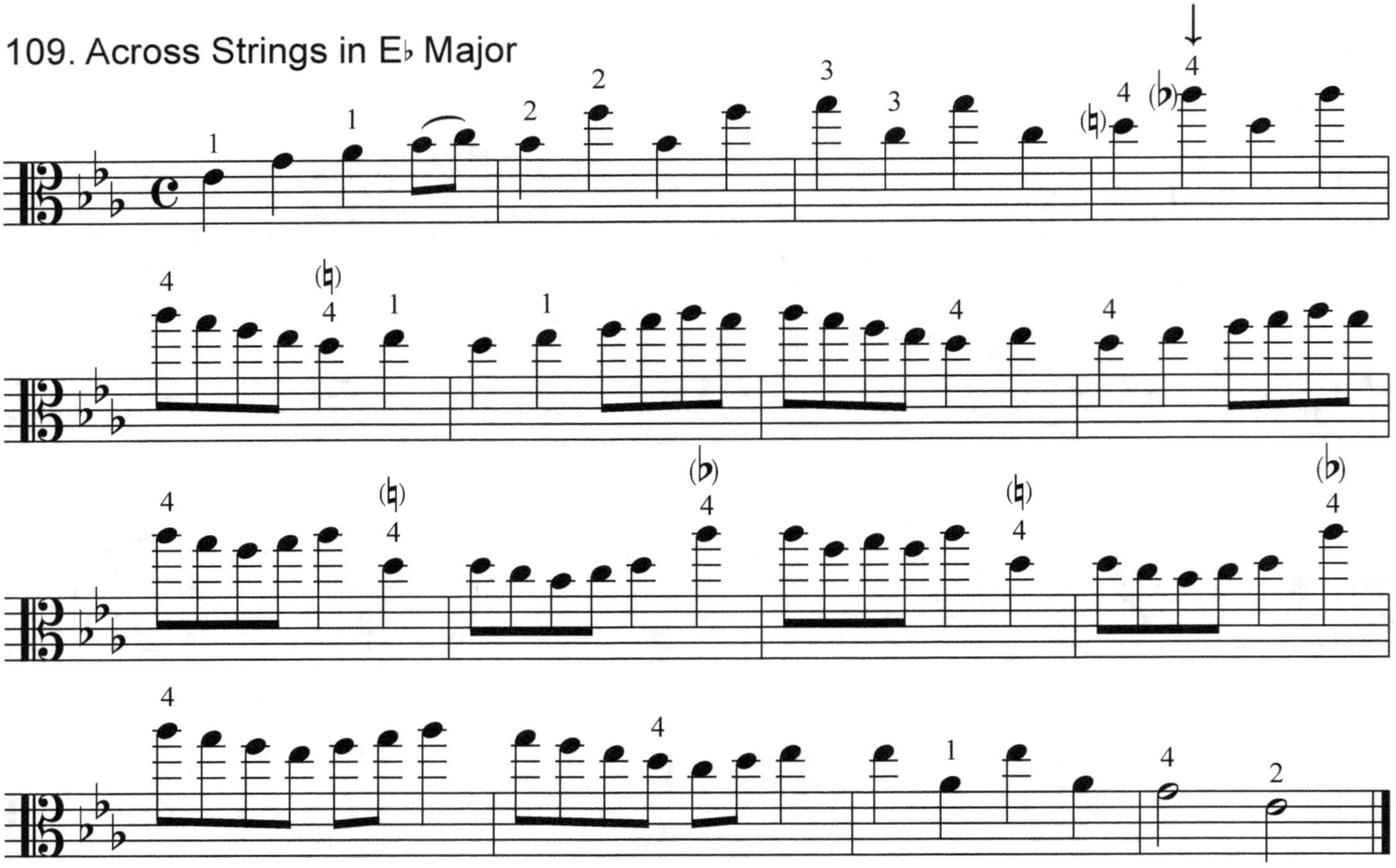

Fourth Position for the Viola

110. Broken Thirds and Shifting

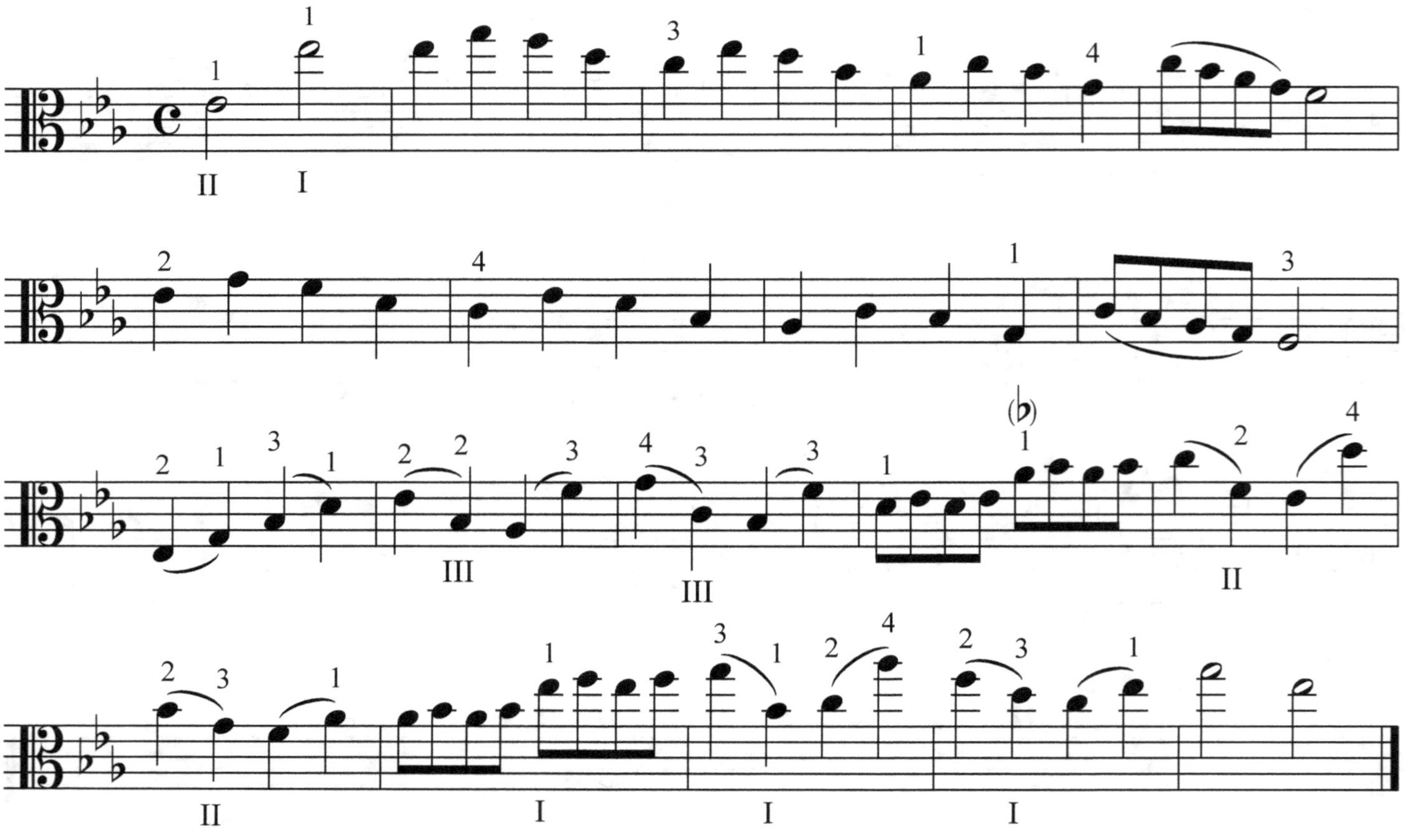

Fourth Position for the Viola

111. Felice

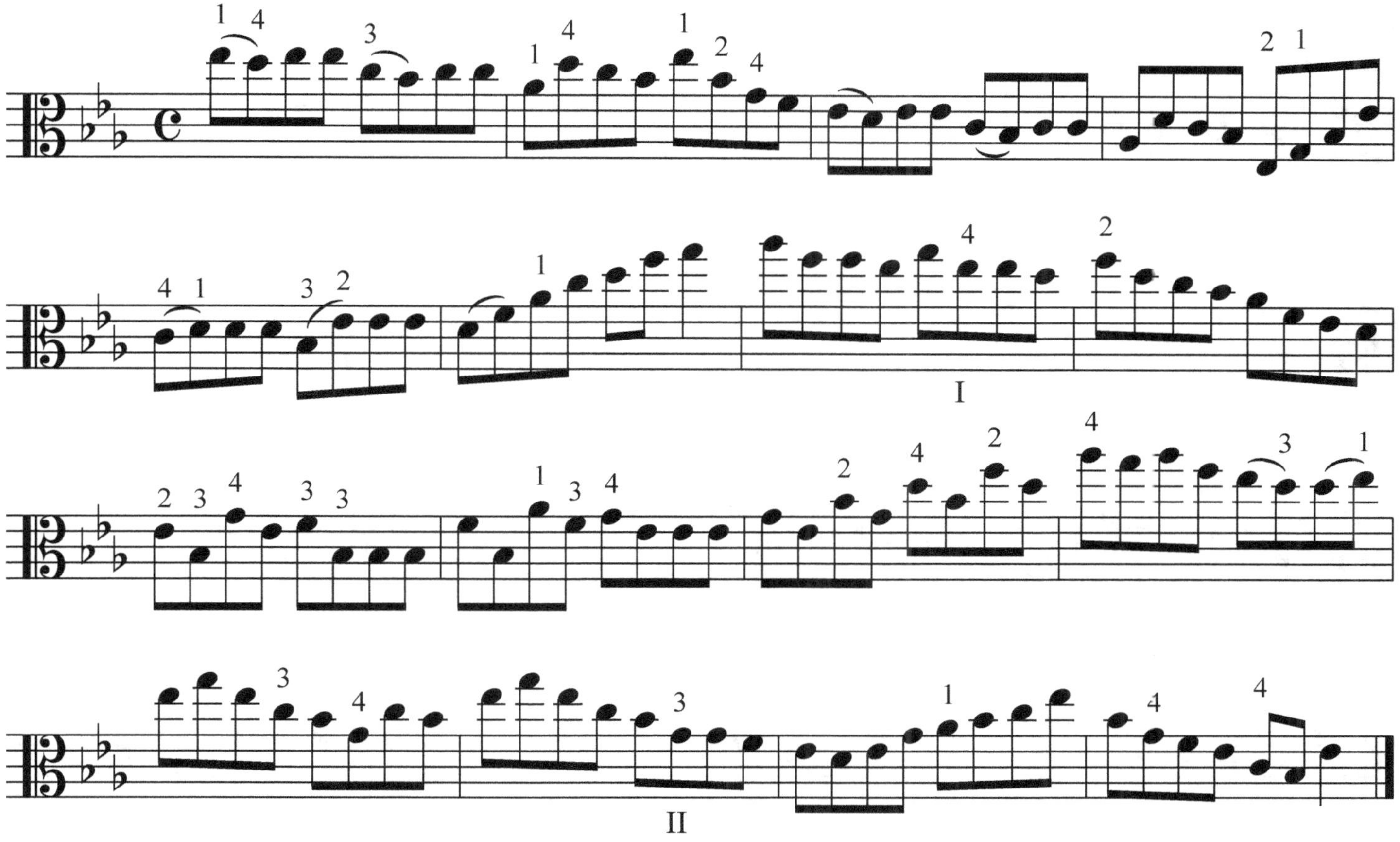

112. Con Brio

113. A♭ Major

114. Finger Patterns on Each String

Fourth Position for the Viola

115. Jasmine Flower; A Folk Song

116. Jack's Maggot; A Folk Song

Fourth Position for the Viola

117. A Pattern in A♭ Major

118. Finger Training in A♭ Major

Fourth Position for the Viola

119. Country Dance

120. Vivaldi's Alla Rustica

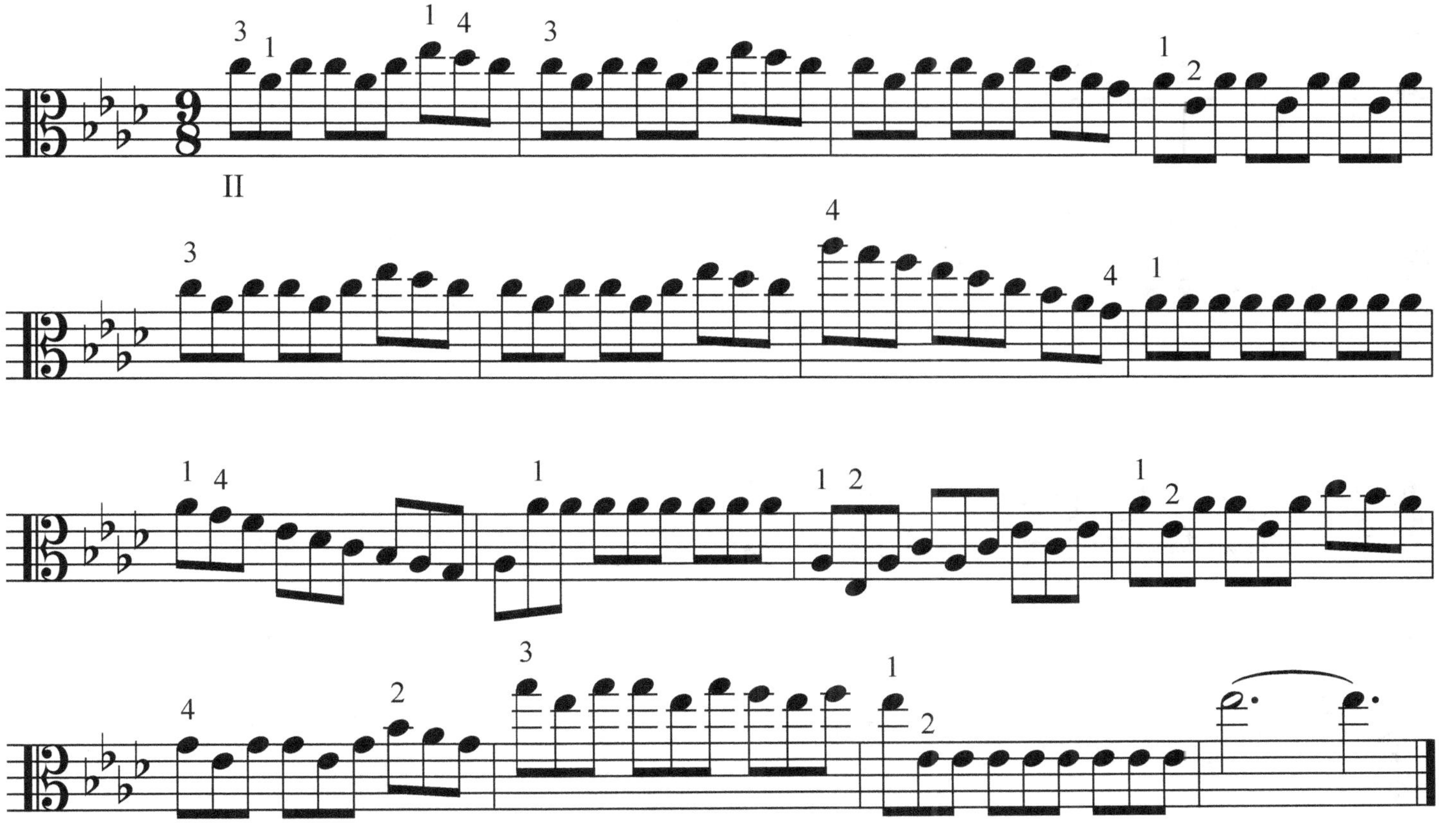

121. Finger Exercise in A♭ Major

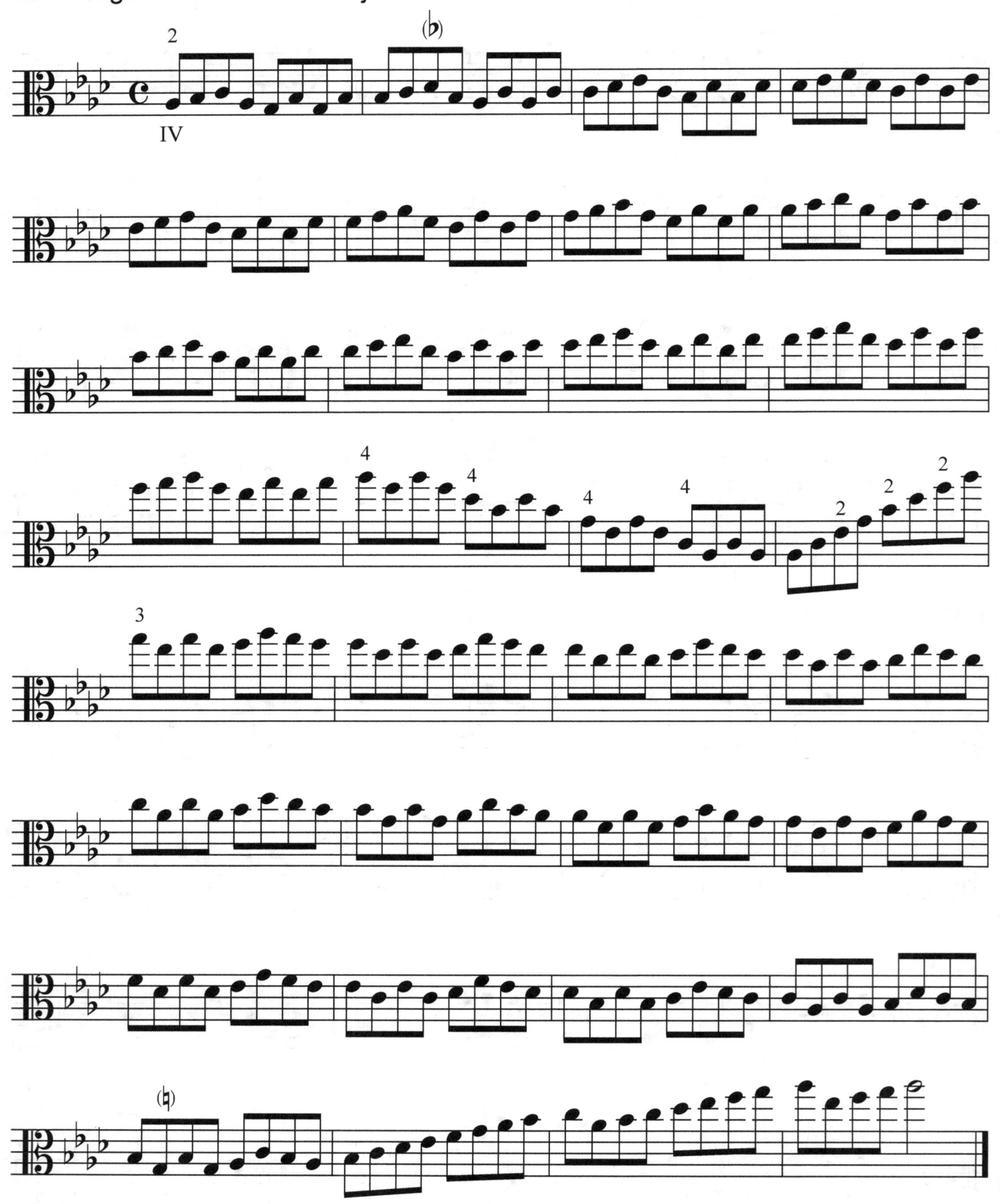

Fourth Position for the Viola

122. Rameau's Rigaudon

123. Tartini's Theme

124. Little Scales That Shift Into Fourth Position

©2017 C. Harvey Publications All Rights Reserved.

Fourth Position for the Viola

70
Fourth Position for the Viola

Fourth Position in Other Keys

125. D♭ Major Scale

126. A Major Scale

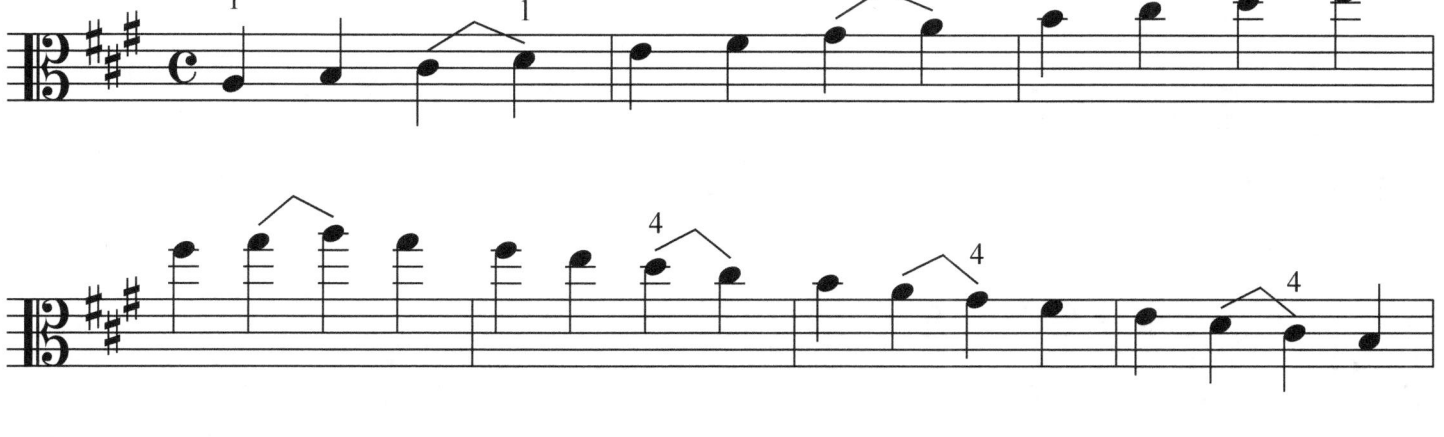

127. A Major Study No. 1

128. A Major Study No. 2

Fourth Position for the Viola

129. March in A

130. Blow the Wind Southerly; a Folk Tune

131. G♭ Major Scale

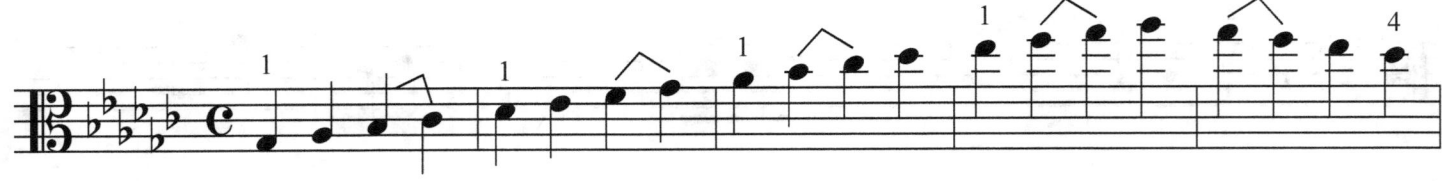

132. E Major Scale

133. B Major Scale

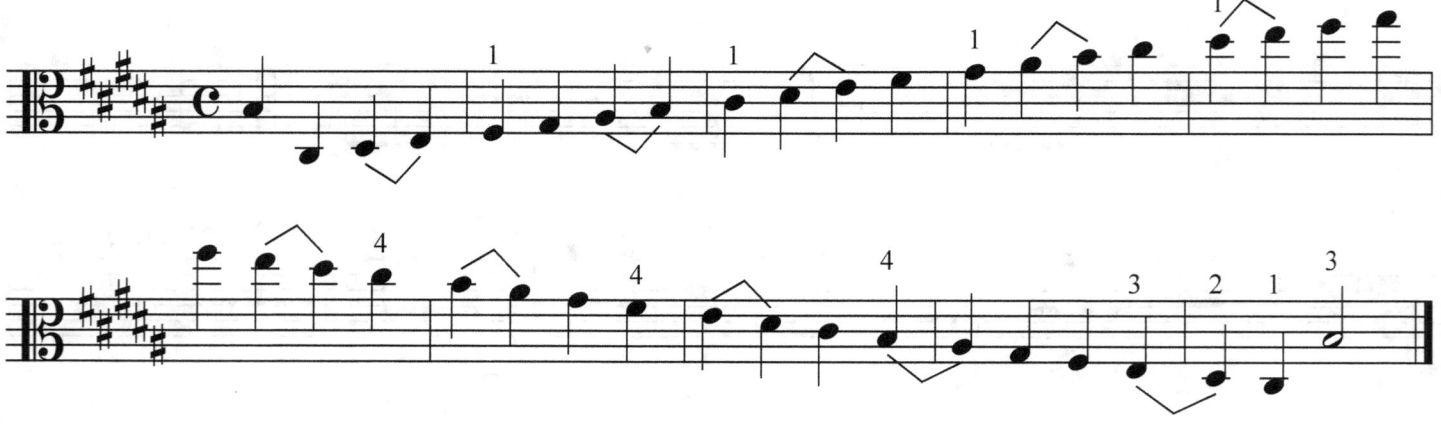

Fourth Position for the Viola

Fingering Chart in C Major

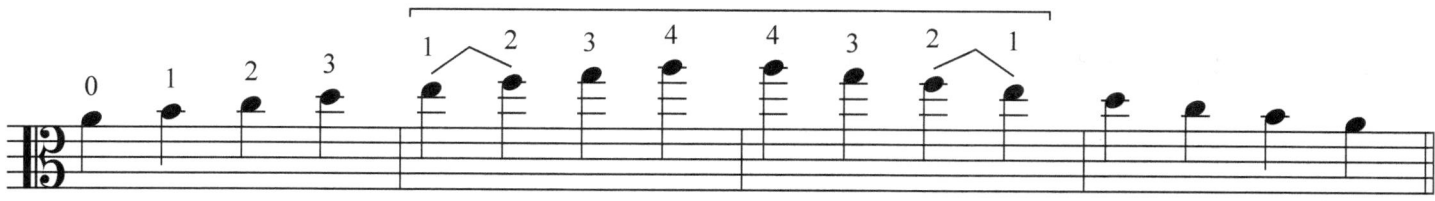
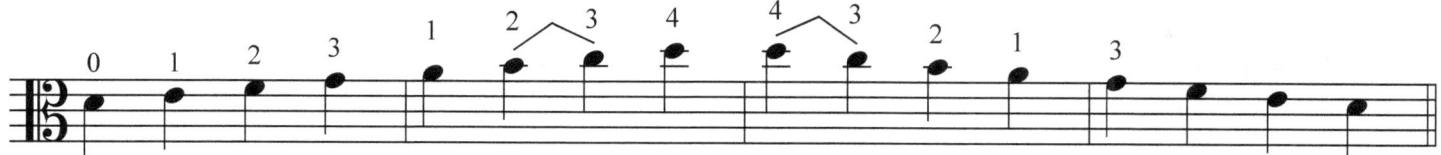

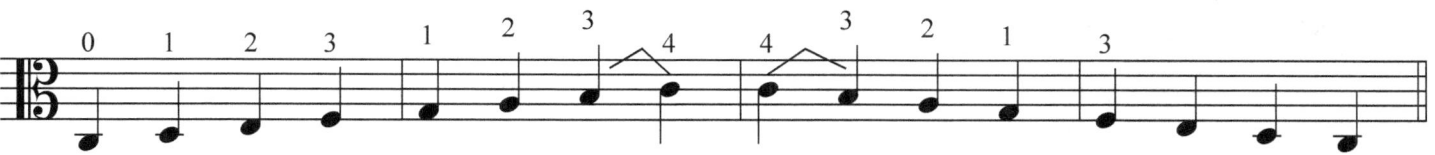

Fourth Position Across Strings

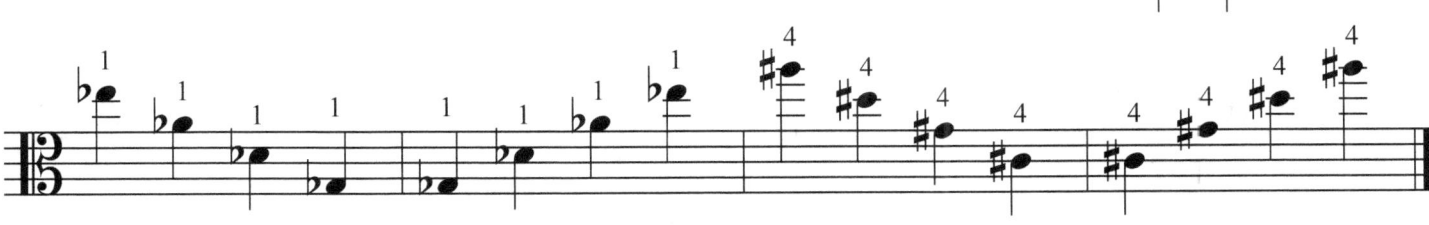

©2017 C. Harvey Publications All Rights Reserved.

available from www.charveypublications.com: CHP173

The Shifting Book for Viola

First to second positions

Cassia Harvey

©2006 C. Harvey Publications All Rights Reserved.

www.ingramcontent.com/pod-product-compliance
Lightning Source LLC
Chambersburg PA
CBHW051422070526
44584CB00023B/3533